Rainbow the Tortoise and His Pot of Gold

Written by Hazel M. Pattison

Illustrated by Wendy J. Rant

Published by Zillah Publishing

This book is dedicated to my family and our dear friend Renee

First edition - published July 2013 By Zillah Publishing, The Cottage, Henley Road, Shillingford, OX10 7EF, United Kingdom

The Author & illustrator assert the moral right to be identified as the author & illustrator of this work.
Story & text copyright © Hazel M. Pattison — Illustrations copyright © Wendy J. Rant
All rights reserved — no part of this publication may be reproduced, stored in a retrieval system,
or transmitted in any form or by any means, electronic, mechanical, photocopying, recording
or otherwise without prior permission of copyright holders.

A CIP catalogue record for this title is available from the British Library

Rainbow the Tortoise© is the brand name for a charitable group raising funds for disadvantaged & disabled people of all ages.
For more information visit our website at www.rainbowthetortoise.co.uk

Rainbow the Tortoise lived with his large Family, in a quiet, sleepy part of Oxfordshire.

Can you see him?

Every day they went out.

Slowly, slowly, 1 2 3, come and have a walk with me.

Rainbow liked to look for food.

Some juicy grass,

some fruit,

or maybe a tasty leaf.

Rainbow and his family like to play with their friends.

Who can you see?

Everyone liked to relax or sleep,   zz   but not Rainbow.

He wanted to know what was outside his home.

Slowly, slowly, 1 2 3,

what is out beyond that tree?

Rainbow liked the stories his Grandad told. Grandad once told him that at the end of every rainbow there was a pot of **gold.**

Where was this?

Could he find it?

How long would it take?

Slowly, slowly, **1 2 3** is there a pot of gold for me?

One sunny spring evening Rainbow had an idea.
He would ask his family to go to different places,
to help him find the pot of gold

He called them to a meeting, down by the potting shed and excitedly told them about his plan. At first they all thought he was being silly but like a tortoise, slowly.........

they began to laugh and chatter

"BUT" said Grandad, it is a great big world out there.

Where will you look?

We can go to the seaside……………………… I can explore the woods……………….

Over the next few months, Rainbow and his family
went here,
there
and everywhere.

Slowly, slowly 1 2 3
please tell Rainbow
what you see.

"Wow" said Rainbow.

This is exciting said Grandad.

Slowly, slowly 1 2 3
I am higher.............

than a Tree.

Slowly, slowly

1 2 3

Is that bluebells

I can see?

Rainbow travelled a long way.

Grandad was right.........

it was a big world.

Would he ever find
his pot of gold?

Rainbow felt sad.

His plan was not working.

No one had found a pot of gold.

Rainbow hid inside his shell

And a few tears rolled down his face

Slowly, slowly

1 2 3

where oh where
can that gold be?

One of the last members of the family to come home was Grandad.
He went slower than the other tortoises,
BUT he was very clever and wise.

Grandad sat down quietly with Rainbow and told him a very, very ,special story......Grandad said,

It does not matter how far you travel, or how quickly you go. As you are a Rainbow tortoise,
with a beautiful rainbow on your
back you will always have your
own pot of gold with you.

Your pot of gold is your kindness and love.
Treasure that you can
share with everyone you meet.

Slowly, slowly

1 2 3

now I'm as HAPPY

as can be.